JOHN THOMPSON'S

FIRST CLASSICS

Contents

Theme from *The Creation* (Haydn) **3**

Can-Can (Offenbach) **4**

Theme from *The Pastoral Symphony* (Beethoven) **5**

Minuet In G (Bach) **6**

Sonatina (Beethoven) **7**

A Musical Joke (Mozart) **8**

"Spring" from *The Four Seasons* (Vivaldi) **9**

"Morning" from *Peer Gynt* (Grieg) **10**

Sextet (Beethoven) **11**

Theme from *The Surprise Symphony* (Haydn) **12**

Theme from *Judas Maccabeus* (Handel) **13**

March from *Carmen* (Bizet) **14**

Theme from *The Trout Quintet* (Schubert) **15**

Waltz (Brahms) **16**

Theme from *The Nutcracker* (Tchaikovsky) **17**

Lullaby (Brahms) **18**

Emperor's Hymn (Hadyn) **19**

Theme from Symphony No.7 (Beethoven) **20**

Theme from *Sleeping Beauty (*Tchaikovsky*)* **21**

Theme from Clarinet Concerto (Mozart) **22**

Nocturne Op.9, No.2 (Chopin) **23**

Bourrée from Music For *The Royal Fireworks* (Handel) . **24**

Theme from *Swan Lake* (Tchaikovsky) **25**

Romance from *Eine Kleine Nachtmusik* (Mozart) **26**

Musette (Bach) **27**

Alla Danza from *The Water Music* (Handel) **28**

German Dance (Mozart) **30**

To A Wild Rose (MacDowell) **31**

"Là ci darem la mano" from *Don Giovanni* (Mozart) . . . **32**

12215

Teachers and Parents

This collection of popular first classics, written in the John Thompson tradition, is intended as supplementary material for the beginning to early level pianist. The pieces may be used by more advanced students for sight reading practice. The material is not specifically graded, although the pieces appearing later in the book tend to be more demanding than earlier ones. Dynamics, phrasing and tempo indications have been deliberately omitted from the earlier pieces, since initially the student's attention should be focussed on playing notes and rhythms accurately. Outline fingering has been included, and in general the hand is assumed to remain in a five-finger position until a new fingering indicates a position shift. The fingering should suit most hands, although logical alternatives are always possible.

The Willis Music Company
Florence, Kentucky 41022-0548

Illustrations by xheight Limited

12215

Theme from *The Creation*

Haydn

12215

Can-Can

Offenbach

Theme from *The Pastoral Symphony*

Beethoven

Minuet In G

Bach

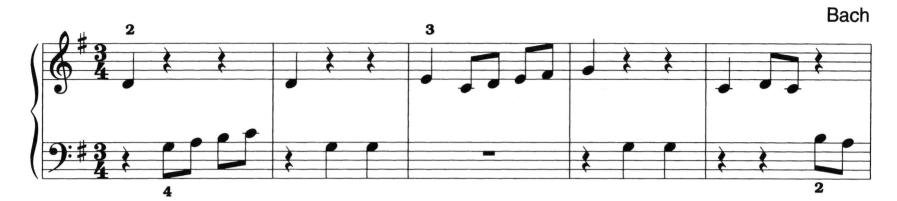

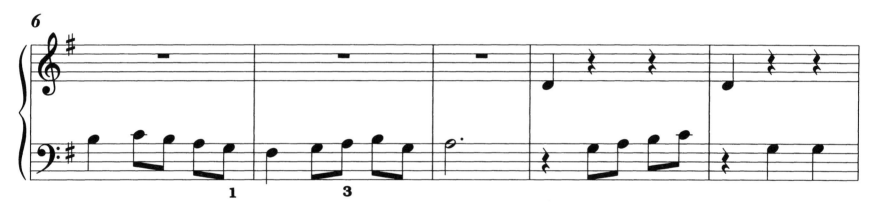

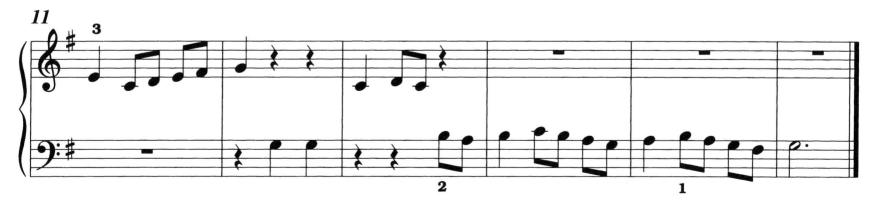

Sonatina

Beethoven

A Musical Joke

Mozart

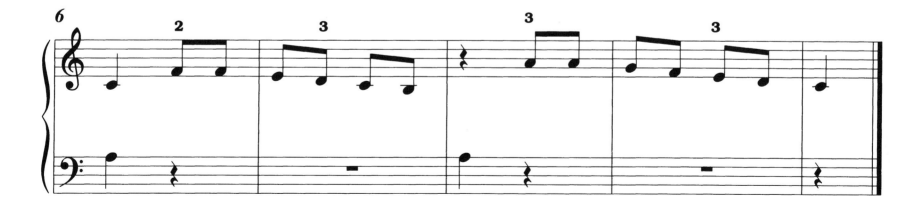

"Spring" from *The Four Seasons*

Vivaldi

"Morning" from *Peer Gynt*

Grieg

Sextet

Beethoven

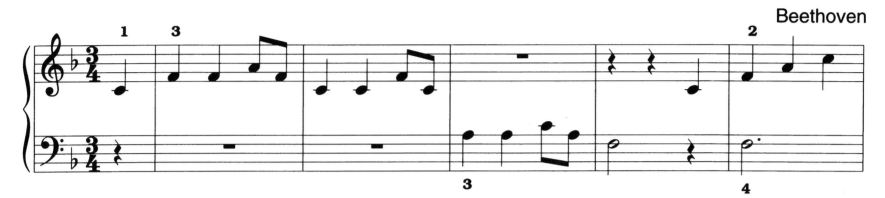

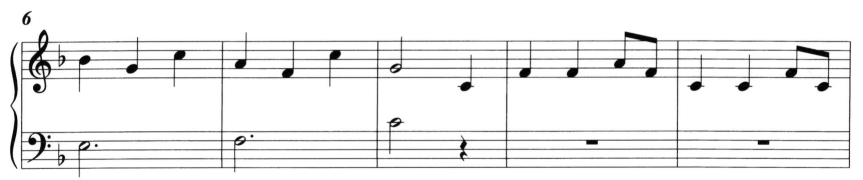

Theme from *The Surprise Symphony*

Haydn

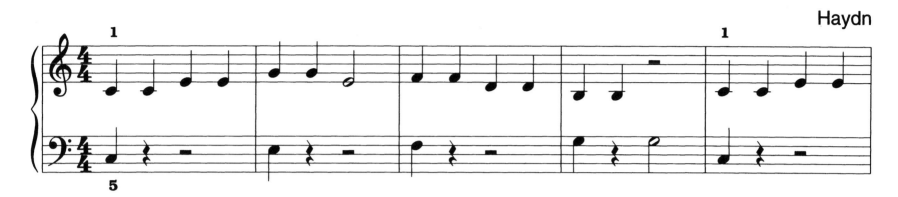

Theme from *Judas Maccabeus*

Handel

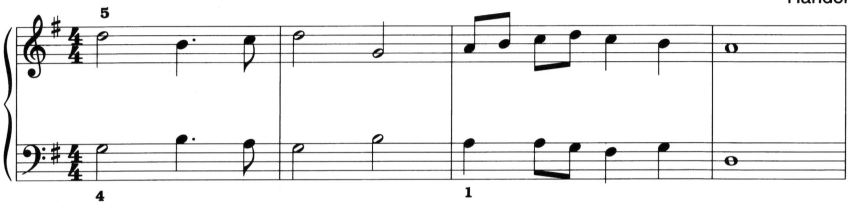

March from *Carmen*

Bizet

Theme from *The Trout Quintet*

Schubert

Waltz

Brahms

Theme from *The Nutcracker*

Tchaikovsky

Lullaby

Brahms

Emperor's Hymn

Moderato

Haydn

Theme from Symphony No. 7

Andante

Beethoven

Theme from *Sleeping Beauty*

Allegretto

Tchaikovsky

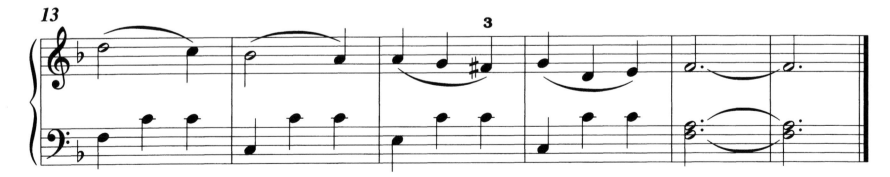

Theme from Clarinet Concerto

Nocturne Op.9, No.2

Moderato

Chopin

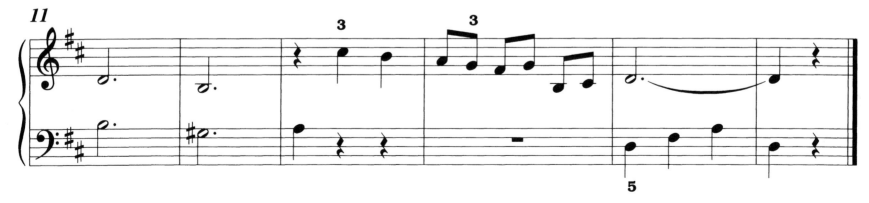

Bourrée from
Music For *The Royal Fireworks*

Allegro

Handel

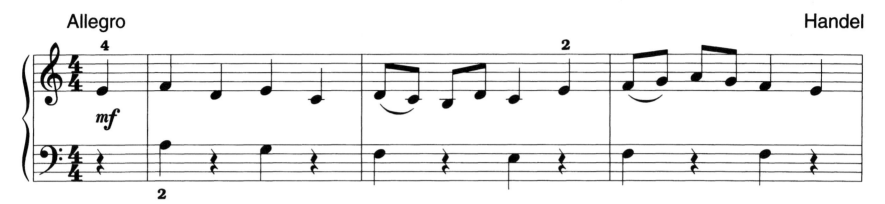

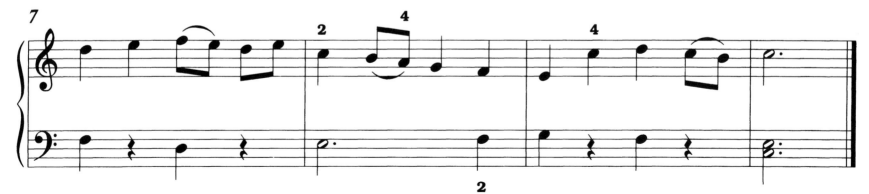

Theme from *Swan Lake*

Tchaikovsky

Romance from
Eine Kleine Nachtmusik

Moderato

Mozart

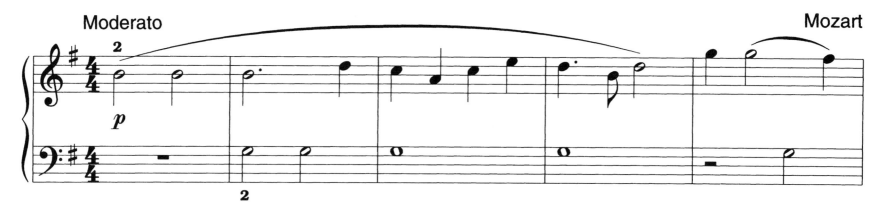

Musette

Allegretto

Bach

12215

Alla Danza
from *The Water Music*

Moderato

Handel

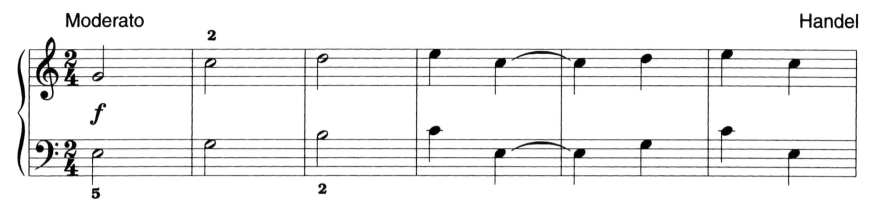

German Dance

Allegretto

Mozart

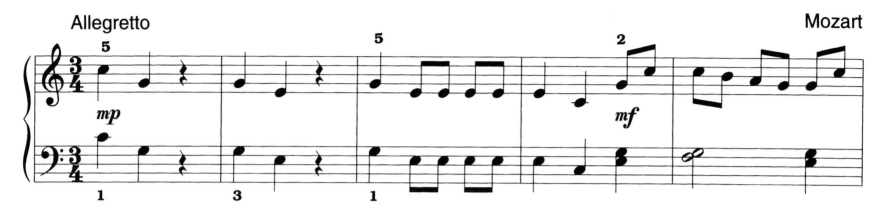

To A Wild Rose

"Là ci darem la mano"
from *Don Giovanni*

Mozart